Brown Paper Wrapper

Free Verse Poetry

J. Coalhouse Lewis

Outskirts Press, Inc.
Denver, Colorado

Brown Paper Wrapper
Free Verse Poetry
All Rights Reserved
Copyright © 2007 J. Coalhouse Lewis
V2.0

Outskirts Press
http://www.outskirtspress.com

ISBN 10: 1-4327-0630-6
ISBN 13: 978-1-4327-0630-2

Outskirts Press and the "OP" logo are trademarks belonging to Outskirts Press, Inc.

Printed in the United States of America

Dedicated to M.C. Crane

Blood

Blood leaking from the middle of the night.. Crimson crimes, burgundy promises. Spilled in the name of self like burgundy wine. Melancholy Merlot races through arteries. Hardened by a feast for the eyes. Admissions of guilt spilled chilled and swirled in crystal glasses. Ruby imprints, liquid flesh peddled processed and refrigerated.

BLACK MINI SKIRT
(Involuntary Manslaughter)

Eyes follow thighs, make you stop....
In mid sentence. Involuntary Manslaughter,
she killed me five times with nightmares
that were soft and wet...
Hemline lost in translation...

Biblical

Cry one droplet at a time
As the gods distill joy from the
Spirits of agony .
Blessings fall short to those living
Upon the cross.
Unsaid vows of poverty
Cast in stone ..

Benny Briscoe's Theory of Flight

Heavy Hands
Touch the Sky..
Dirty fingernails
Conceal a prizefighter.
Under street lights,
Alley-way persuasion..
Heavy-Hands collect
Sunday dinner left
To rot on the curb.
Shadow boxing combinations
Punch Drunk Wisdom
Keep Heavy Hands
Higher than Eddie Kendrick's
Falsetto, fisticuffs strike wind
Left jab taps the chin...

Motor running on salty
Egg whites, Hot sauce
And the sight of
Another man's fear
Taking a Heart without
Surgery, jus stitches.
Sparing with the
Heaviness of being
     A
   Lightweight.

Bailey St.

Geto children play barefoot among the diamonds. The bottoms
of little feet black from the soft asphalt. Imagination is a
doggie sayer as a committee of kids hold down the steps
outside. Future girlfriends in the bloom of sexuality dance in
the street. Grinding fresh hips to a beat produced by hand claps
and foot stomps. While a captive audience looks on with eager
new erections. Schools out, heat melts each hour of daylight.
Around the way cool torrents of water gush from the fireplug.
Grab a bucket, wet or be wet. Joanie with the big butt creates
water peacocks by sticking her ass in the fire hydrant. The
afternoon cool down has begun. Screams of splash victims'
echo up and down the block. Grand Master Flash and the
Furious Five celebrates the night with drumbeats and bass.
Controversies of the day simmer and boil over into evening.
Darkness creeps in among the oldheads patrolling the corner.
Providing cover for the pungent sweet smell of reefer, and its
cousin Wild Irish Rose in a brown skirt. After the third game
of hide and go seek is played, mothers call for the youngsters.
Gentle breezes stroke the tops of trees, god sings Bailey st. a
lullaby, parents reclaim the steps and porches.
Sipping beer they reminisce, the years that sped by, the
summer of 68' ringing in their ears..

A Bird in the Hand
Beats 2 In The Bush

50-caliber diplomacy paper democracy one nation over-god
evangelize, with cruise missiles, laser guided policy. Dropping
ordinance on ordinary casualties, countries colonized by the
dollar. Dance to the doctrine of manifest destiny, Tonkin
resolutions. Patriot Acts of Desperation placating with
placebos under the table. Extortion on a dollar bill better still
Ben Franklin. 50 caliber diplomacy paper democracy riding
shotgun with righteous indignation, a white man's burden. A
bird in the hand beats two in the Bush
Clinton sin on CNN. Bush sly like a Fox news live. The truth
lies on airwaves, save me from myself. Concrete cascade 9/11
fades into a national holiday. Oh say can you see the
Flag draped bodies they don't want you to see.

Mumia, Fate and a 45'

Truth stuck in his throat. Reporting black facts to blacks beaten blue. Mumia fate and a 45' caught by a thin blue line. Brother's keeper kept on maximum security ice. Calmly living to die by lethal injection of payback, state assisted homicide. Breathe his last breath, taste his tears; keep his secrets. Hesitant star of a one-ring circus. Underglass for underclass, fame made dirty by a shot in the dark. Innocence revolving around a revolver. Prosecution rests on Chestnut St. reasonable doubt lay in a puddle of warm riddles. Fate and a 45'. Present tense turned past tense in 1/16th of a second , no second chances. Bullets have no conscience, no memory no mercy 50 lashes of white backlash leave welts. Mumia, fate and a 45' no nolo contendre, no deferred adjudication. Asking back blood from anger. His name infamous in spray paint. Whispered and Shouted in holy high frequencies. Beyond the range of soothsayers, doomsayers political game players who shoot dice with public opinion. Roll snake eyes. On death row. Mumia fate and a 45'

Momma

When pop ran off, we cried, you didn't.
Knees sore, knuckles raw, from days
Work. We seen your eyes too.
We love you.

Miles Davis is the devil

Finger tips tap on three keys..
Hot. Like butter in a skillet..
Play a note, He'd kill it.
Light a cigarette with no match..
Giving the mind something sticky
and sweet to bite down on..
The music plays long after the record
stops...

Menthol Kisses

Filtered Menthol flavored favors plead mornings forgiveness. Thin rubber membranes replace sensation like conversation rambunctious and lubricated. Shots in the dark, screaming orgasmic operas in octaves higher than Pavarotti. Switching hot breath inside momentary paralysis.
Nocturnal Emissions.

Mattress Dancer

Mattress dancer, bedspring queen, leaving the best part of man
on cotton sheets.
On her back since 13. Daddy don't !! Vaginal initiation into the
red light
District. Street walking against traffic, tit & ass dress
packaging pleasure.
Providing 5 seconds of relief, release. Tricks pushing hard
manhood into
Petals of lost soft womanhood. Stroking the males dick and
ego until he
Shoots his 3rd or 4th baby into a latex baby catcher. Leave the
twenty on the
Dresser. If this is sin, who is the transgressor. Love is not sex,
sex is not love
Some love to have sex, mattress dancer what's next, mattress
dancer what's
Next.

Lipstick

Lipstick on the Edge of midnight. Cognac tinted secrets lie to you, or down with you. Words hang motionless, floating, on first impressions. Being what the moment lacks forget-me-nots argue with pillow talk. 2 o'clock in the morning selective amnesia sits cross-legged, running her fingers through last night. Ez terms, transparent kisses, temporary sincerity provide mood music for the games people play. Touching glasses mesmerized,. Breast to chest between heartbeats, borrowed emotions based on mechanical motions... This is for those who sleep alone...

LAWD JESUS
Notes on Hurricane Katrina

Lawd Jesus, the sea done knocked on my door..
Angry waves razor sharp teeth chewing on undigested
promises, under handed gestures, open wound festers
In the corners of idle minds...

Lawd Jesus the sea done knocked on my door..
black waifs wonder, black waifs wander like refugees,
lost in the ninth ward, speaking the unspoken "ism".
Race takes place when black is the face, that familiar
stranger. White collar crimes of passion produced a
shotgun marriage of the " haves and the have nots"
leaving illegitimate children with no last names..

" for you have the poor always with you, but me you will not
always. "

John 12: 8

JACK JOHNSON
THAT BAD NIGGER
1878-1946

Fist philosophy beat Mister Charlie's pink face
Master race laid low. Right cross set crosses
a fire. Bad Nigga did'nt look away boy, look away.
Skin like midnight, white girls delight,
inside a Dixie menage a trois...
Intergrating Jim Crow's underpants.
Victim of circumstance dance in the squared circle.
Bad Nigga painted bourbon colored canvas red,
slap boxed the devil with negritude..

INMATE # 14127739

Ms. Brown, carrying 9 months of fear
9 months of pain, 9 months of expectations.
Expectations, expectations. He smiles like his father
Before the armed robbery case. He cries like his mother
In the middle of the night. Saving her sanity looking
Into brown eyed brown skinned miracle, miraculous, magical
My son, my son. Little boy brown how long will it be before
you learn to get down.
Be down
Lay down
Stay down
Way down
Taken downtown in handcuffs.
Bastard by incarceration facing general population only 18..
Little boy brown how long will it be before you
Break down
Bow down
Go down
Down low
On his knees giving bulls a blow job for blow.
Name taken, ass taken, manhood taken, faith shaken
Shaking, in the middle of the night,
He cries like his mother…

Heroes

Heroes hiding in six glass zeros
Superstar status
Media apparatus
Manufacturing Heroes,
for those who fiend for self-esteem
Be like Mike
Be like Mike
Can I get mine,
If I'm 6'9".

GUNPLAY

Caress the barrel, feel your steel, so hard, hard forever,squeeze, with a quick twitch watch the tip spit death 16 times, until the pee hole smokes, Nine millimeter dick, waiting for the urge to steal lives the morgue is full of lead overdoses. Leftovers from a Saturday night special. America obese on a high fat diet of gunfights, and body counts, brought to your living room on 82 channels.
N.R.A. has a choke hold on gun control, Government has sold its soul, because dollars make sense. Channel X broadcast daily casualties, only thirty seconds of reality, and now for the sports. Since the revolution witness the evolution of violence. The color of blood woven into the flag. As we place our hands over our hearts. Warfare rages on the back pages of yesterday's newspaper. Imitating Massa's game of right by might. Peace looking down a rifle sight...

GRACE

By the grace of God they stared at a one eyed Raven .22 and
seen the next day.
By the grace of God they slow dance, pressing up against
supple lies,
lifeless mannequins stare heavenward. Your name on their last
breath...

GetoSpeak

Contradtion in fiction calling phonics Ebonics. This ain't
fiction , AEIOU/pronunciation E-enunciation social
stratification unholy geto words find their way to the suburbs-
white folks ask why? Why try to classify thoughts lifted from
The young black and gifted, C. Delores Tucker missed it, the
language of the cotton field. When talking proper could get
you killed African Semantics caught in Colonial Cross Hairs-
every sentence a Hy-Breed of a Dirty-Deed

FEMININE
DELICASIES

Slurping like oysters on the half shell....
Making my nature rise with bedroom eyes...
Teddy Pendergrass playing close the door...
tongue kissing your internal thermometer...
As I lay, face down in your universe....

EULOGY FOR RON O'NEAL
A.K.A SUPERFLY

125th Harlem perspires beneath white wall tires, European
headlights
show the way. Pushaman selling stepped on fantasy.
Pharmaceuticals not found on shelves, found on the New York
stock exchange.
Exchange in Central Park, when it's dark.
Pushaman, salvation comes in the witching hour,
White powder is white power sedate Negroes with skag.
Walk between raindrops superfly, its raining in Harlem.
Bump toe San Remo's move to Curtis Mayfield's lament.
The good Lord hangs on a wall to the forsaken.
Pushaman, mainline opiate aspirations like new religion…
Pushaman kilograms killaman, kilograms killaman…..

DOWN BY LAW

The gnarled hands of my people, are as the deep ruts and grooves of the mangrove. Lines that trace lives back to its origin. Veins that pumped thick crimson blood into rich Georgia soil.

Coupe Deville or Coup Deta

(Bloody Revolution)

Peanut Butter colored leather highbacks. CD changer pounds premium sounds conditioned air, 5th wheel in the rear. Windows limo tinted, don't stare, don't stare suspension/suspended in Cabrini Green/diggin the scene with the gangsta lean. Rollin' the luxury penitentiary, penthouse, outhouse, big White House. Handouts on Jesse Jackson's clout. Creature comfort sedates higher learning, striving for higher earning, Mississippi still burning. Black sheep wear fleece on their backs, drowning in a salty sea of complacency, power steering, steering around potholes called confrontation, fuel injected acceleration; leaving Kwame' Ture', Marcus Garvey, and Steven Biko in the slow lane, paid full sticker price with ill gotten gains. Of what price is fame? Of what price Assimilation? Of what price Integration? Coupe Deville or Coup Deta' ..

Blue Dahlia

In the seam between midnight
walks a stranger. New to the fractures
In the mirror, only seeing the insides
Of eyelids, living in the shade of blue light.
Surrounded by good wars,
Artificially flavored truth. Melting, mixing
Conscience and sub conscience into
pop culture.
Force fed forced smiles
Until reality is a figment of the
Imagination.
Starvation with a belly full of sweet
Nothings.
The spin cycle hangs dirty laundry
Out to dry…

Bob Beamon's Theory on Speed

Sweet Georgia clay clinging to heels. Breathless, on the run
700 miles. Paying the last installment on a slice of apple pie.
Paid with sandpaper hands of sharecroppers. Picking the pride
of the Southland. Refusing to whistle Dixie, Eye wrestling
racist red faces. Colored boys swing, meaning swung, colored
boys got hung, for soiling panty-white Hysteria. Run Nigga,
Run Run past 16th street Baptist church; Run past Bull
Connor's German shepherds. On legs of Bob Beamon leap 29
feet into the future. Piston-like movements Powered by
boycotts, Buckshot's, nightsticks might stick to your ribs,
Semi-Automatic intentions. Condolences leave Exit-wounds
natural track stars run to silent applause. Only the sound of a
body striking wind at the rate of 100 meters in nine seconds,
speed….

Broad & Lehigh

Standing on the corner, at Broad & Lehigh the world in your hand.
Escape cooked up and crumbled inhaled, on sale.
Standing on the corner, women get down to get high, high like
The first time. Police play game wardens, protecting game.
Standing on the corner, men on missions look for their sanity
Under the streetlight, as ribcages show under skin...

Correctional Facility

Warehouse factories, 103 degrees producing hard heads. Bang, cell-doors all night long reminding you that when you open- your damn eyes you will see bars. Cellblocks put black faces on shelves, black faces become numbers. Three hots and a cot in exchange for your mentality. Generations of numbers walking the yard. This systems bad sons in a rage too potent for the streets. 8'x4' purgatories mumble stories of what could have been. Faded Polaroid's form an inheritance. From fathers to sons, as mother and daughters point and say- "That's your daddy."

The Derelict

Peasants Dream as kings lying upon this night's pallet. Kings dare not dream, for they live fantasies. A poor man's vision of grandeur passes through the night as the sidewalk dies. Dreams lend fire to an old, what used to be blanket. Closing the eyes tightly to behold what this world denies

The Patient

Notice the lingering cough from a 400-year-old malignancy.
Only symptomatic to those borne of the middle passage. Empty
remedies trickle down IVs flooding veins with the by-products
of great society. Famished from the remnants of America's
titty.

Doctors, with masks on inject 500 c.c.s of mind raping
assimilation with a morphine base. Inject 1000 c.c.s of Re-
education causing hallucinations of equality. Inject 200 c.c.s of
religion administered by a sad faced Jesus. The white coats
extract soul, astounded, confounded at this fluids resiliency.
Purity surrounded by the profane.

Doctors offer a negative prognosis with cold steel pressed to a
heaving chest. The subject is not responding to our treatment in
arrogant ignorance. They overlook the patient's allergic
reaction to their prescription.

A nation with no country has taken ill. Malnourished and
weak, but refusing to die. Our medicine is of our own making;
next 400 years will be a very bitter pill to swallow.

Suga-cube,
Confessions of a one Nightstand

Suga-cube sweet coating on four-sides called emotions going through motions. In and out of passing glances, looking to see whose eyes are the deepest. Pressing my index finger to your lips dare not say a word. Whispers in the dark, fade into falsifications fabrications. Saying what must be said to get you Horizontal. Hot Sweet liquid rolling down arched backs trying to liquefy your suga-cube. The point of no return Turns Bittersweet, the 8:30 checkout seals the deal. Suga-cube. All that remains is the sugary essence, as the lies, can I's echo in a Playa's fantasy....

SPARE CHANGE

Brotha, can you spare a dime, piece of mind, chump change?
Change me c-h-a-n-g-e me metamorphosis, morph larger than
pocket change. Substantial like gravity. Rearrange me more
than two syllables. Transform from guilty to fat free freedom.
On sale for spare change. Nickel and dime lip service makes
change for a dollar. Change the smirk on George Washington's
face. Change me with platinum shackles. Arrived, but going
nowhere, on borrowed bus-fare, what's fair? Rain dance for
copper rain, inside the oxblood deuce and a quarter, quarter
vinyl avenue cruiser, Dime dropping on penny-pinching pigs in
blankets, who can't make change who can't make change,
change into
A progress pimp, limp step, put change on the ho-stroll.
Changing minds behind dumpsters, in backseats, backstreets.
Change yesterday, make it theme music for a black and white
drama, featuring Dark Gable. Change pain into wine; get drunk
off the illusion. Can you spare some change Can you spare
some change, some change.

SIN

Drink Ice cold stilettos with maraschino cherries from the inner thighs of big bottomed girls, who want to fuck the world. But got fucked by the world. Society flies by at the speed of Dolby Digital light. Seeing god on Motel ceilings. Worship skintight altars, in sequined Halters. Sin formed in the womb of willing customers, sin pushed out in blood flecked badness. Pushed around in strollers. Synthetic love sold by the pound, in tamper-proof packages. Watch tomorrow today for 49.99 a month..

Shank

I lay beside the knife, prison shank, blink it becomes a 12"
butcher knife.
I'm not blessed I guess I'll get dressed in Sunday best and slit
my wrist.
Beat fate to the punch, in the holy book Christ died for my
sins.
In that case I've stabbed Jesus with wrongs never made right.
Stabbed with a prison shank 12" butcher knife.
Visions of the blade cuts through my night dream,
Making the night scream at the sight of unholy blood.
I lay beside the knife, feeling the chill of cold steel,
Wondering if God listens to my appeals.
His youngest son sleeps lightly.
The razor sharp edge of reality sleeps in my bed.
Separating love from hate in a heart that beats for two
Masters. I lay beside the knife, kiss the blade as she shaves
Off layers of life.
Doing my dance on the point of a prison shank, 12" butcher
knife…

Say Cheese

Say cheese, don't smile when you say it.
Cheese more than a dietary staple.
You need cheese to pay your rent,
At the end of the month, you say damn,
That cheese was well spent.
L.B.J. had Vietnam, Nixon had Watergate,
Reagan beat them all with a 5 pound paper
Weight.
I hate to be fowl, but too much cheese
Can stop up your bowels.
Ask Clarence Thomas who needs to wipe
His lip, he ate a plate full of queso dip.
Just to get a date with a blind white
Woman, whose scales need to be
Recalibrated. Clarence sits on the supreme bench,
Constipated. The bougies are cheese eating
Connoisseur's, they prefer their cheese on
Crackers, like that famous actor,"everything
Taste better sitting on a Ritz".
NAACP if the shoe fits.
Say cheese, but don't smile when you
Say it. Eating cheese to make cheese,
On your knees, say please.
We all can't be G's …
Some of us attend universities,
Fortune 500 employees,
Sitting on committees,

Driving sport utilities,
Living in gated communities.
Ignoring racial hostilities.
Can you be black without
Changing the way you act ?
Snack on that Monterrey Jack for
Change that lines your pocket.
Say cheese,
But don't smile when you say it..

Seeds

The sun never finds us seeds as we lay as pods underneath fields of sorrow. Forever patient, dormant, incarcerated in the dark earth. Waiting for a chance to blossom in Jah's light. Only now confined to the grounds vault. Locked away trapped inside her seeds lie suspended in fields of sorrow.

SACRAMENT

Masses partake mass, holding the father, the son, and the holy
ghost under tongues.
Speaking in tongues of dead Latin verses. Kiss the ring of pope
on a rope, washing
Silk, mohair, cashmere robes white with the blood of heathen
natives, who never
Realized nakedness. Feed us Jesus in small pieces, filleted ,
without bones of
Contention. Content to use his name in vain, vanity genuflect
over stolen gold.
Prepackaged pagan deities with manmade halos stare
heavenward.
Selling grace to disposable sinners, palms pressed together in
pious
Dread of fire an brimstone moans. Through tight lips men of
the cloth
Bless armies in the name of God and country, country and
God.
Sending boys to private crucifixions losing limbs in shell
shocked
Epiphany. Pulpit politics on Sundays praise God manufactured
by
Middlemen, amen, said at the end of broken prayers.
Bowed heads, mourning the silence and distance of God..

PRECIOUS

Your thought process is precious, when soul is manifest, in the
fire of black hearts. I am a practitioner of the black arts, not
hocus pocus get your mind to focus on the fire you possess.
With fresh bloodstains they tried to tame the flame. Riding the
wings of Jim Crow, fanning smoldering cinders of those who
remember culture thieves. Who stole original knowledge and
called it philosophy. Inner Light hold with all your might.
Faceless ghost tries to separate this fire from soul, swinging
from a tree cold. Evil man take away my body you can't
destroy soul. Soul that makes me lean when I drive. Soul that
gives Rhythm to my walk. Man seeks to extinguish the fire-
patrolling streets with guns for hire. Cold eyes betray jealousy
envy, and hunger. Hungry, for that warmth inside me, but this
personal inferno burns internal. Remember your thought
process is precious when soul is manifest, in the fire of black
hearts.

PAM GRIER

The nature of a chocolate Venus. Nipples like buttons on a
bronze goddess.
May I knell before your temple, fleshly gates open. I will bless
you, the way you blessed me. Her touch makes nights hotter
than Tunisia, as I lay covered in the sweat of my own exertion.
Kisses wet me until the pleasure closes my eyes. Is this a
dream, or has fantasy made love to reality. Desire drowns
rational thought. Possession is my obsession in the darkness of
the bedroom. Subconscious hands caress her soft form in
angelic repose. Morning comes as a thief, standing in the
shower; questions run down my face like water mixed with
tears. Spent emotions swirl and disappear.

Northside

Check the street; know only the eyes that look back at you. On the sidewalk, blood drops in silence. Spent Newport's die slow. View the jungle from the sidewalk.

12:00 am

The sun feels bright against closed eyes. Open up to the morning, a new day to soak in the light before it goes dark. After dark we hold court. Proceed with the bad, actions prove a man worthy. Wait for the new day to end the darkness, to feel the warm sun-on our faces. Before long it will night. Be afraid, we know our deeds.

No Tears Formula

Body owned by fate. Embraced by the last words of a mother, whose hollowed out veins contain street medicine. Holding close the sound of stolen sex. Hustlers pawn small lives, for big gold chains. A face the color of blank canvas, wingless white flight. Gritty reminders left in hieroglyphic Graffiti, Civilization, uncivilized. Asexually nude, alabaster shoulders, wearing the streets like a black Mink stole. Day dreaming of 5th avenue, standing in Hell's kitchen. Baking chocolate chip wish cookies. Mining for one night's treasure, fooling her-self not her stomach. Malnutrition rubs against backbone. Yesterday leaves an aftertaste. Rapid eye movement keeps the night at arms length. Drinking virgin Martini's made of tears and Vermouth. A smile concealed under 1 inch of bulletproof skin. Teflon coated girl raised on blasphemous neon lights. Triple X, hard core, 100 proof life.

New Orleans

Sip brown colored fire water intoxicated by blind
Musicians. Howling in syncopation, rhythm produced
By bucking hips musty and natural. Backroom phantoms
Move under covers. Moans make strange music inside
The ears of voyeurs who look and touch themselves
Vicarious soul claps stolen from the badlands,
Killing fields, ghettos.
Smile a Louis Armstrong smile.

Working Man

The day cast its shadow over me …
Carrying weary bones into evening….

Wilson's West Philly Barbeque
John Africa's Ghost

Wilson Goode gave John Africa a drop of water to cool his,
parched lips, as he sat Indian style in a man made Hades. This
mass cremation is brought to you live, by the Philadelphia-
Police Department. They prefer their revenge seasoned with
shellcasings. Smoldering dreads became incense to the nose of
Mr. Sambor inside the round temple of violence. He laughs as
he washes his-hands blood red from the children of Africa.
10,000 rounds of ammo equals 10,000 reasons to die, nigga
why? Baptism by fire, the unwilling sacrifice perished in the
artificial hell named West Philly

Warlocks with M-16's prodded mad, black Angus to the fire.
When the smoke ascended from the altar on Osage Avenue,
Wilson bowed down facing the fire and gave the Devil his due.
Don't worry children, do not weep, the Devil made him do it.
Lucifer invades his sleep at night showing glossy color 6x 9's
of the burnt offerings. His eyes weary from the torment of the
ghost of John Africa, Don't worry children do not weep, there
are no refunds on his soul, all sales are final.

We are the KIN

We are kin to the darkness. We well know the night. As others shun the dusk, we relate to the moon on a cloudless evening. Kin to the darkness of night.

WALLOVENS

Summatime transforms row homes into wallovens.
Black folks sweating, marinating, waiting for that
12:30 ripple in the air. Corner congregations pose
with their nostrils flared.
Defiant to a blast furnace of a July Friday night.
Porches house refugees from the sun's
Oppression.
Anticipation beads and runs down shiny foreheads.
At 1:15 Jah whispers, permeating the air with
His cool blessings.
Now the third world can sleep....

US

Hold soil in the gold studded mouths of complete strangers.
In danger of losing a limb in of a war without walls.
Forced isolation on the tip of the tongue of bigots with
Digits. Graceful cannibals who enjoy finger sandwiches.
As we sit down on plastic chairs, eat on paper plates.
Drink from Styrofoam cups, all shit that gets thrown away
After the party.
Listen to complete strangers taught to forget names,
Remember faces , tell good lies in thirty minute intervals.
Make us smile slap our knees and wait for the punch line.
Us , stacked five deep, making love to recycled beats,
Grinning through clinched teeth. Clicking African
Sounds reverberate, speaking to people, anonymous like
Hotel soap that never seems to clean your fingernails.
Blackmailed black males can't afford bail, massa build
Bigger jail. Some dwell in split level hell, air conditioning their
Psychosis. Goosestep to constitutional cadence right wing
dreams of white
Christmas caused by soft money, soft core, safety sealed for
your protection.
Political prostitutes in blue suits ride low on the hog….

"Under Cover"

Her, Him, He, She, he graduated from chicks to dicks AKA-
Boy Pussy don't call him cum-snatcher he pitches not catches.

She looks in the mirror and sees a she-male not female. She
has a taste for feminine delicacies. Pink-Panties and pearl,
tongue she knows Victoria's Secret.

Unda cova luva's of others. Others who like a strange taste in
their mouths…

The Three M's

Brotha Martin climbed the mountain he looked around and saw
he was alone. The Promised Land missed us. Brotha Marcus
just wanted to go home. Back to Africa, he found his people
too material; we buy Jordan's like cereal. Brotha Malcolm
taught, there no me just us, building our own is a must. Did he
figure a nigger would pull the trigger? Why do we taste blood
after daring to dream? Still living in tarpaper shacks. Do we
lack direction, Affection, or somewhere down the line did we
lose God's protection? His-story and the future kicks my ass.
The past got whipped and hung from a tree not far from my
doorstep. The present is virtual reality, virtual homicide, virtual
genocide, and virtual suicide. I get down on my knees and
pray. Please jah, let me slide. Please jah, let me slide.
Nobody's on my side. 400 years in the missionary position has
left us neglected, injected, infected with white sperm, white
germ. Trying to make my brown eyes blue, these eyes reflect
the evil that men do. They tell me I should be happy. In fact
you can sit anywhere on the bus. Goddamit, I want to drive the
bus, then swerve to hit the Bell curve. Voices, voices in the
dark, voices in your head, the ghosts of the good ol'days hides
in our memory. Until the vomit of rage spews from our lips.
Cursing our life, Cursing our birth, when life alone is the
sweetest fruit in the garden. Sometimes we kiss ourselves up to
God. Asking for what no man can gives us. Going insane, up to
my neck in a game playing on the outside looking in with my
nose pressed against the glass. Is this my imagination? I pour
my rage into a shot glass, throw my head back a swallow hard.

Rage burns in my chest. Burns like crosses. Burns like rosewood. Burns like Newark. Burns like Watts. Burns like South central. Burns like Osage Avenue. Burns like Liberty City. Racial instability raises the ghetto's flammability, ashes to ashes in a fucked up reality. Oh no can it be the true criminals of society has to keep an eye on me. Deep down inside they know my capability. Castration economically deeps the boot on our necks. Massa keeps black schizophrenia medicated with 40oz dreams pseudo-equality schemes. As we endure the long journey from so-called barbarian to African American.

The Fall of Lower Case Gods

Lower Case Gods
Fell 186,000 feet
Per second
In a Heartbeat
Blink of an eye
Precipice-Abyss
Hit plate glass
On your ass freeze
If you move
I will separate you
From your Brain waves.
Jail instinctive thoughts
Make you dance buck-wild
In Technicolor cages
cursing cotton candy
Prayers. Falling-failing
To maintain Equilibrium.
Delirious from a Thousand
Moons, a thousand
Tombs Death come
Too soon.
Unspeakable acts
On the Backs of Blacks

Strip mine minds
For Archeological finds
Leaving craters
In the pupil of
Your eyes.....

The White Lady

Cocaine, the 500 million-dollar white lady. Not too elegant to sleep around the geto. Which is fueled by the white standard. Fives and tens change hands from the addicted man to the pusha man. Goddamm, he just brought a lex coupe, paid cash. Compliments from the white bitch.

Coke and her sista crack compromized, capitalized, and sodomized black love. I look over my shoulder in my hood cuz I don't know who has an oral fixation for the inhalation of ready rock. Peanut, she used to be fine, now she stoops down in dark alleys. On the business end of somebody's business. The flava of dick goes nicely with the taste of base, what a waste, find a good lawyer beat a dope case.

This triple beam queen likes to be sexed in many ways. Chopped up fine and snorted. Heated up and injected, or crystallized. Realize this bitch will get inside your head. Taking niggas to 60,000 feet, droppin' them in the free-fall with no parachute. Droppin' in a drug related emaciated hell of Jonsin' for the next high.

Hey rock-star, does hits on a pipe give you 15 minutes of fame, or 15 minutes of shame. Pimped in a game where the players live in far away places. While Peanut's baby cries on a piss-stained mattress, fiend'n because Columbia flows through his tiny veins. Niggas can't seem to get enough of the lady's French kiss. As they say, just say no. The white lady walks the streets. As they say, just say no, the white lady owns the streets.

Revenge of the New Negro

I seen that NEGRO hanging from a tree
I seen that NIGGA hanging on a bedroom wall
In middle America, in the middle of a white girls
Chocolate fantasy.
I seen that NEGRO pushing plows through cotton fields.
I seen that NIGGA pushing Bentleys from NFL playing
fields
Million dollar field hands, hands clap for superstars
Shooting stars with hoop dreams of becoming a new
NIGGA.
I seen that NEGRO step and fetch it.
I seen that NIGGA go and get it.
One step ahead of Uncle Ben, Aunt Jemima, and the latest
"urban comedy" on the WB.
I seen that NEGRO shot in the back with a shotgun blast
I seen that NIGGA snort white dust for a mega blast
High enough to remember past, NEGRO nitemares of
Dred Scott, Nat Turner, and separate but equal bleeds
Into the here and now.
NEGROS and NIGGAS caught by their toe, invisible
limbo
Transform into mannish boys 22 inches higher than
Chrome rims spin, new NIGGAS spin wheels of steel
Making music from the pain of one drum.
Listen to your heartbeat…

Mary's Bossa Nova

Six strings sing.. Coaxing notes from air, conjuring the
daydreams of Favellas.
Making love to conga drums, beating them into
submission.
Pluck chords, unlock padlocked rhythms that escaped from
sugarcane plantations.
Slender fingers tease black saints stolen from Africa.
Mary sings from her stomach, someplace deep inside,
Finding her voice with a beautiful noise.
Like the distant memories of an old chanteuse
Mary's Bossa Nova touched tan hips persuading
Bodies to move to and fro, like strong magic…

Untitled

Once my skin matched up against the sky..
Ebony fighting streaks of red sunlight the speed of dawn
found me at Angkor Wat
Interrogating statues who smile a Mona Lisa smile.
They knew me well, whispering, this god made of human
hands told me
I witnessed the birth of Akhenaten and wept at the death of
the sun.
Vowing to wait for the son of man like a pregnant bride
holding sins in her belly.
Making slaves of those who skin bore evidence of the
eclipse, children of the first
Sunrise, children of the first night. Lost I found my self on
a trans Atlantic conveyor belt.
Chained to the lies that lie inside me.
My skin matched up to whip marks leaving unmarked
graves
Slaves sing at their own funerals.
I remember that song…

Printed in the United States
83109LV00002B/1-9/A